Maximizing Church Growth

When Leaders Utilize
the
Power of Spiritual Gifts

Claudia B. Hawkins

Printed in the United States of America
Copyright © 2021 *Claudia B. Hawkins*

ISBN: 978-0-578-91869-3
Publisher: Claudia B. Hawkins

WEBSITE: www.ethicstrainingandconsulting.com
EMAIL: claudia@ethicstrainingandconsulting.com

DEDICATION

I dedicate this book to…
my Lord and Savior, Jesus Christ, who is everything to
me;

my father (deceased) who was also my first pastor, who
loved the Lord and his family, preached the Word, and
served his congregation;

my mother (deceased) who was my first teacher and role
model of a Proverbs 31 Woman;

my sons, Omar and Rashid who inspire me to be the best
Christian mother I can be;

my grandson, Malik; and extended family members and
friends; and to my three major church families of
Macedonia Baptist Church in Darlington, SC; Triumph
Baptist Church in Philadelphia, PA; and Grace Temple
Baptist Church in Lawnside, NJ.

ACKNOWLEDGEMENTS

I am thankful to:

God for saving me, loving me, and placing this desire in my heart to write this book for His glory;

My family and friends who have loved and supported me over the years;

Pastor James Hall, Jr. for preaching that confirmed my salvation as an adult;

Pastor Quincy and Arnetta Hobbs for their friendship and encouragement to discover and utilize my Spiritual Gifts;

My Biblical Editor, Rev. Dr. Henry T. Simmons; my Advising Editors, Dr. Cecilia Dennery and Giselle Ogando; my Content Advisor Arnetta Hobbs; and Language Advisor Candice Davis - all for their expertise, guidance, and patience.

To God, Alone, Be the Glory!!!

TABLE OF CONTENTS

INTRODUCTORY QUOTE

"Nothing on earth compares to a group of believers in a local church, under the control of the Holy Spirit and using their divinely given gifts to minister to the body. The body then builds itself up in love. When growing in unity, truth, and love; a lot of problems take care of themselves, before they become big, because the body is healing itself. A healthy body, working as designed, will grow and every member will benefit."

Author Unknown

CHAPTER 1

WHY SPIRITUAL GIFTS

This book is written to encourage all new and not-so-new Christians to identify their Spiritual Gifts and then serve in them enthusiastically and passionately. Why? Because many people join a church and never realize that they have Spiritual Gifts; what their Spiritual Gifts are; and how much better a church can operate when everyone is serving in their gifts.

Many church leaders introduce Spiritual Gifts at their New Members Orientation. This instruction should include the definition of Spiritual Gifts, the types of Spiritual Gifts, and then the comparison of those Spiritual Gifts to acquired talents or skills.

According to the Zondervan Pictorial Bible Dictionary, Spiritual Gifts "is used in the New Testament to refer to extraordinary gifts of the Spirit given to Christians to equip them for the service of the church. Several lists of such gifts are given…. They may be broadly divided into two categories, those connected with the ministry of the Word of God and those connected with the ministry of practical service."

Spiritual Gifts are a gift from God through the Holy Spirit at the time of our salvation. We may not recognize our gifts immediately, but they are there. It is a calling God has placed on our lives to perform a special service in the church. We must find out what they are and know that we must use them in service to our church for the glory of God.

God is so gracious, and He gives us more than one gift. Knowing your predominant gift is important because it will make you more effective and will give you an increase of joy and peace when you utilize these gifts in service to your church ministry.

For example, if the gift of serving is your primary gift and you are spending most of your time using your gift of teaching, you are not using your gift in the most effective manner. I am not saying that your teaching is not a blessing, but we know that the Holy Spirit is to guide you to what is best and not just what seems better (John 16:13). We should not get involved in too many different ministries because the dominant gift and the various ministries will suffer. This means the Holy Spirit's anointed gift to us will not be operating at its maximum capacity. I have been guilty of that.

What happens in a church where there are not

enough members to serve in one needed ministry? A call will go out for volunteers. Will you volunteer if that ministry does not align with your dominant spiritual gift? We find that, if there are not others to serve in a particular ministry, you may volunteer to serve in a secondary gift for a season. However, in prayer, be alert when God sends new people to your congregation with that gift and encourage them to get plugged in to their dominant spiritual gift.

Also, if your secondary gifts are needed in your current church, you may use them there for a time. Later, if you relocate to another church, look for the ministry that will benefit the most from your dominant spiritual gift. Again, you will be more effective, more joyful, and more at peace in that ministry. Expect that ministry to grow when members are serving in their anointed and appointed gifts.

Spiritual Gifts should be compared to acquired talents or skills so that new believers will know the difference. A talent is a natural ability or aptitude. A skill is the ability to use your knowledge to execute or perform an act, task, operation, etc. Talents can be inherited. You know many families who have musical talents. The whole family can sing and play different instruments. They may end up forming a family musical group that goes on to become world renowned, like the Clark Sisters, the Staple Singers, and the Winans.

Skill is different in that you may have an inherited ability, let's say in athletics; and yet you must use your knowledge and ability to maintain and improve those skills to compete on a national stage. God gives skills as well and this is chronicled in Exodus 36 which tells us about Bezaleel and Aholiab and other skilled craftsmen who had the knowledge and understanding to perform work on the sanctuary.

God gives us the Spiritual Gifts to use specifically in the work of the church. So, take for example a teacher recognized as "Teacher of the Year" in your public-school system. Should that person be allowed to teach Sunday School? Yes, if that is a lay skill as well as a spiritual gift. If it is not a spiritual gift, the teacher will not be as effective and the students may not be nurtured, nor flourish as they would with someone who is called to teach.

The Biblical editor that I used for this book is a longtime family friend and a retired pastor. I know him to be a great preacher and administrator who is also a wonderful artist. I've never heard him play but I am also aware of his abilities as a musician and founder of the Jazz Vespers services at his previous church. This shows that God truly is gracious, and we can have more than one spiritual gift, as well as talents and skills that must be maintained and practiced.

Do you have wonderful talents and skills as well as multiple Spiritual Gifts? Well, take this opportunity to have a 30-second praise party to the Lord for His generosity toward you. Remember specifically that your Spiritual Gifts are to be used to glorify God in your service to your local church.

We do not need to be jealous of anyone else's gifts since God is the perfect giver. He knows the best gifts for you and everyone else. He knows how He wants you to use it for His special glory, that no one else can do but you. Every spiritual gift is needed to make the church operate to full capacity. That does not happen when we covet someone else's gift instead of maximizing our own gift.

Apostle Paul, previously known as Saul, is the author of thirteen of the twenty-seven books of the New Testament. I will be referencing many of his books in the following chapters. So, we can certainly look to him for counsel on how we need to use our Spiritual Gifts. He writes to the Galatians in Chapter 5:22-26, The Message Version to say:

22-23 But what happens when we live God's way? He brings gifts into our lives, much the same way that fruit appears in an orchard—things like affection for others, exuberance about life, serenity. We develop a willingness to stick with things, a sense of compassion in the heart, and a conviction that a basic holiness permeates things and people. We find ourselves involved in loyal commitments, not needing to force our way in life, able to marshal and direct our energies wisely.

23-24 Legalism is helpless in bringing this about; it only gets in the way. Among those who belong to Christ, everything connected with getting our own way and mindlessly responding to what everyone else calls necessities is killed off for good—crucified.

25-26 Since this is the kind of life we have chosen, the life of the Spirit, let us make sure that we do not just hold it as an idea in our heads or a sentiment in our hearts, but work out its implications in every detail of our lives. That means we will not compare ourselves with each other as if one of us were better and another worse. We have far more interesting things to do with our lives. Each of us is an original.

Verses 22-23 list the fruit of the Spirit: love, joy, peace, patience, kindness, goodness, faithfulness, gentleness, and self-control. Fruit here is singular because it describes the character of Christ. Christlikeness is the fruit made up of all nine virtues. We will supernaturally display and portray that fruit when we serve in our Spiritual Gifts, as received from the Holy Spirit. That means we are using our gifts with God's heart, from a humble spirit. When we think of how holy God is, and then for Him to allow us to be His hands and feet to grow the Kingdom, that is really an "Oh my Lord" moment! He's using me?!!!

Verse 24 tells us that the law cannot miraculously help us demonstrate love, joy, peace, etc. The Holy Spirit lives in us to transform us to feel the love, joy, peace, etc. as we are serving in our Spiritual Gifts.

With the spiritual fruit and Spiritual Gifts working together, we exhibit that we are living and following the Holy Spirit. There will be no conceit, provocation of others, or jealousy; as Paul writes in verses 25-26, to conclude this chapter.

The less obvious or less public the gift is does not make it any less important for the ultimate work of each function of the church. God is no respecter of persons, therefore the duties of a janitor are just as important as the duties of the deacon when done in love, humility, and honor to God.

Most church leaders should understand God's plan for the use of these gifts in the church. Favoring family members, large donors and/or long-time family members to serve in specific high-profile ministries is not God's desire for growing His church. When we place the emphasis on matching the member's spiritual gift to the ministry, we alleviate man's flawed desires, and we follow God's intentions.

Another thing to consider is, if a new member arrives with a dominant spiritual gift that is not needed for any current ministries, maybe God is saying this could be an opportunity for a new ministry or outreach. At every turn in reading and understanding Spiritual Gifts and other leadings of the Holy Spirit, prayer and meditation should be sincerely and passionately pursued to see what God wants done in His local church.

Wisdom is still crying in the streets per Proverbs 8 saying, "I am what you need, wisdom." Those on your leadership teams with the Inspirational Gifts of Wisdom should be consulted to join in prayer for the direction and alignment of the Spiritual Gifts with the appropriate ministry.

Following up on new members after a certain specified time to see that they have connected to a ministry matching their gift will go a long way in growing your church.

Church leaders really need to have an intentional

and strategic process to get members involved in observing, then serving in ministries soon after joining. Why do you think God gave us these gifts if He did not want us to use them? When church leaders complain about the 80/20 rule (80% of the work in the church is being carried out by 20% of the membership), do they think to ask why this is? I have no doubt in my mind that two of the reasons are because our members are not serving, and others are not serving where they are anointed to serve!

A Gallup Poll article written by Jeffrey M. Jones, April 17, 2019 reports,
"U.S. Church Membership Down Sharply in Past Two Decades." The story highlights that:

1. Half of Americans are church members, down from 70% in 1999.

2. Most of the decline is attributable to increase in percentage with no religion.

3. Membership has fallen nine points among those who are religious.

So herein lies another reason for those who are already members to know what their gifts are; and, for those who will be coming and returning to learn what their Spiritual Gifts are. The church will be a more impactful, vibrant, growing, and effective organism, when more members are serving in their God-given Spiritual Gifts. We must continue realizing that it's all about exalting God and not ourselves.

My objectives are to:

    1) provide scriptures from the Bible about Spiritual Gifts,

    2) identify each type of spiritual gift,

    3) discuss each motivational gift in detail *and*

    4) inspire you to identify and use your gifts for the glory of God.

There are three particular scriptures in the Bible that fully relate to Spiritual Gifts, although others reference them. They are Romans 12:6-8, I Corinthians 12:7-10 and Ephesians 4:11-13. Here are excerpts from all three:

Romans 12:6-8 KJV

6 Having then gifts differing according to the grace that is given to us, whether prophecy, let us prophesy according to the proportion of faith;
7 Or ministry, let us wait on our ministering: or he that teacheth, on teaching;
8 Or he that exhorteth, on exhortation: he that giveth, let him do it with simplicity; he that ruleth, with diligence; he that sheweth mercy, with cheerfulness.

I Corinthians 12:7-10 KJV

7 But the manifestation of the Spirit is given to every man to profit withal.
8 For to one is given by the Spirit the word of wisdom; to another the word of knowledge by the same Spirit;
9 To another faith by the same Spirit; to another the gifts of healing by the same Spirit;
10 To another the working of miracles; to another prophecy; to another discerning of spirits; to another divers kinds of tongues; to another the interpretation of tongues:

Ephesians 4:11-13 KJV

11 And he gave some, apostles; and some, prophets; and some, evangelists; and some, pastors and teachers;
12 For the perfecting of the saints, for the work of the ministry, for the edifying of the body of Christ:
13 Till we all come in the unity of the faith, and of the knowledge of the Son of God, unto a perfect man, unto the measure of the stature of the fulness of Christ:

The Bible answers why we are given Spiritual Gifts…to help each other and for the common good. Some of you may not remember when we receive these gifts. We receive these gifts when we accept Jesus Christ as our Savior. They are placed in us. The Spiritual Gifts are not a feeling we get when we receive them, but once we know what our gifts are, we do have a warmth and joyful feeling when we serve in them.

How can you find out what your gifts are?

1) You can pray and ask God to show you what your gifts are;
2) You can remember what gives you that special warmth, joy, and fulfillment when you are serving others;
3) You can listen closely when family and friends compliment and encourage you as you do special things for others; and
4) You can take a "Spiritual Gifts" assessment.

Today, there are many online Spiritual Gifts assessments to help you determine what your Spiritual Gifts are. This is a great place in the book for you to go online and take one of the many Spiritual Gifts assessments that exist. They may be referred to as a Spiritual Gifts test, survey, questionnaire, or assessment. No matter the name, take one or more. When you finish and read about the motivational gifts, you will begin to discern what God placed in your heart when you accepted Him as your Savior and Lord.

CHAPTER 2

TYPES OF SPIRITUAL GIFTS

The scriptures refer to three types of gifts. They are Motivational Gifts, "Proclamational" Gifts, and Inspirational or Manifestation Gifts.

Romans 12:6-8 identifies Motivational Gifts. These gifts are given to us by God as a motivation for us to serve.

Prophecy	Ministering/ Serving	Teaching
Exhortation	Giving	Ruler/ Administration
	Mercy	

Ephesians 4:11 identifies the "Proclamational" Gifts. These gifts are given to certain people by God to proclaim God's Word.

Apostles	Prophets	Evangelist
Pastors		Teachers

I Corinthians 12:7-10 identifies the Inspirational (Manifestation) Gifts. These gifts can be seen in a believer as he/she operates in a particular situation.

Words of Wisdom	Words of Knowledge	Faith
Healing	Working of Miracles	Prophecy
Discerning of Spirits	Diverse Kinds of Tongues	Interpretation of Tongues

The purpose of this book is to discuss the Motivational Gifts that are to be used by the saints to build, operate, and maintain the church ministries as it provides for the needs of its members, the lost, the property, and the community.

CHAPTER 3

THE GIFT OF PROPHECY

The first spiritual gift we will cover is prophecy. What do you think of when you hear the word prophecy? A revelation? Something that is predicted to happen in the future?

The Free Dictionary.com defines prophecy (the last syllable sounds like the word "sea") as a noun that means a prediction, the inspired utterance of a prophet. On the other hand, to prophesy (the last syllable sounds like "sigh") is a verb which means to speak as a prophet; to foretell future events.

From a Biblical perspective, prophesying is the primary job of a prophet. God calls a prophet and tells him what to share with the people or with one person. The prophet will share something that nobody else knows, others are unable to foresee or discern. It will be a surprise when it is shared. To make it a true prophecy, it will come to pass as it was foretold.

Some prophecies in the Bible have already come to pass, others will come to pass soon or in the not-so-near future.

Prophecy can also mean that the person knows the truth of God and speaks the truth of God with power and passion. These we know as our preachers. They proclaim the truth. Most pastors and preachers will say that they have been called by God to be a preacher. This is not an easy calling and they must spend much time studying and meditating on the Word of God so that they may be able to explain or rightly divide the truth that people need to hear.

A few scriptures in the Bible that refer to prophecy are listed below. You should study them more if you think this may be your gift.

Deuteronomy 18:21-22 NLT

21 "But you may wonder, 'How will we know whether or not a prophecy is from the LORD?'

22 If the prophet speaks in the LORD's name but his prediction does not happen or come true, you will know that the LORD did not give that message. That prophet has spoken without my authority and need not be feared.

Joel 2:28-32 NLT

28 "Then, after doing all those things,
I will pour out my Spirit upon all people.
Your sons and daughters will prophesy.
Your old men will dream dreams,

and your young men will see visions.
29 In those days I will pour out my Spirit
even on servants—men and women alike.
30 And I will cause wonders in the heavens and on the
earth—
blood and fire and columns of smoke.
31 The sun will become dark,
and the moon will turn blood red
before that great and terrible day of the LORD arrives.
32 But everyone who calls on the name of the LORD
will be saved,
for some on Mount Zion in Jerusalem will escape, just as
the LORD has said.
These will be among the survivors whom the LORD has
called.

2 Peter 1:20-21 NLT

20 Above all, you must realize that no prophecy in
Scripture ever came from the prophet's own
understanding,[h] 21 or from human initiative. No, those
prophets were moved by the Holy Spirit, and they spoke
from God.

How do you know if you have this gift? You
cannot remain quiet when you hear false Biblical
statements and principles!

Yes, prophecy is a spiritual gift, and everyone
does not have this gift. When this is your gift,
you study and meditate on the Bible. You know
of prophecies that have come to pass, so when
you hear someone say something contrary to that

prophecy, you cannot keep quiet. The same strong will to say something overwhelms you when you hear an inaccurate prediction for the future, too. You again cannot keep quiet, when you hear a misrepresentation of the Word, a lie, or a deceiving accusation.

For example, if a person were to say that he completed massive computations and came up with the date of February 1, 2025 to be the end of the world, the person with this gift would immediately counter that true prophecies come from God. See 2 Peter 1:20-21. Knowing this is a truth, he can preach this lesson in a sermon for people to be alert to those who claim to be prophets but are not. The Bible states in Matthew 24:36, no one knows the day or the hour.

In proclaiming the truth, those with the gift of prophecy/truth-telling are concerned with identifying ways to spot false prophets. There are certain things the Bible commands us to do, therefore a person promoting these commands as options should be shunned. What if a new preacher moves into your community and teaches that you really don't need to forgive your enemies? This would really irritate the person with the gift of prophecy because this is not a Biblical truth.

Some of the people in the Bible with this

spiritual gift were Peter, Abraham, Moses, and John the Baptist.

Peter. Peter was the most famous of the twelve disciples. Why? Because he was the leader, the most outspoken, the short-tempered one, the most combative. He felt himself to be the most committed. We see Peter speaking up in the book of Acts, words received from God that were spoken by the Prophet Joel. God revealed to Peter that Ananias and Sapphira had lied about the gift they brought to the Apostles in Acts 5. Peter's name is mentioned first whenever the inner circle is named in the Bible...Peter, James, and John. Even after denying Jesus three times, he is allowed to deliver the Word on the Day of Pentecost, where three thousand souls were saved. There are so many interesting stories about Peter as a prophet and leader of the 12 disciples.

Abraham. What do you already know about Abraham? Most of us know that God promised him that he would be the father of many nations; that his name was changed from Abram to Abraham; that he and his wife Sarah were both very old when God promised them a son; and that they did have Isaac when they were 100 and 90 years old respectively. God kept His promise and today Abraham is considered the father of the Israelites, the Ishmaelites, the Edomites, the

Amalekites, the Kenizzites, the Midianites, and the Assyrians. The first time we see "prophet" in the Bible is in Genesis 20:7 where God Himself calls Abraham a prophet. Abraham is in sin in this story as he has lied to the heathen King Abimelech, telling him that Sarah is his sister. God came to the king in a dream, before he had touched Sarah and told him he must release Sarah, and that Abraham was a prophet. Obeying God, the king and his people's lives were spared.

Moses. Moses is known as the most famous prophet of the Old Testament. He received the word from God to give to Pharaoh for him to release the Israelites from slavery. Although it took ten plagues to finally get Pharaoh to release them, it happened. In the wilderness, Moses received the Ten Commandments from God, twice. Moses is known as the prophet to Israel in addition to being the deliverer, the leader, and the lawgiver.

John the Baptist. John the Baptist is the cousin of Jesus as you may remember. When Mary found out that she was pregnant with Jesus, she journeyed to visit her cousin Elizabeth who was also pregnant at that time with John. John the Baptist is known as the forerunner to Christ because he prophesied the coming of Jesus as he preached in the wilderness. His prophecy was to repent because the Messiah was coming.

The characteristics of persons with this gift are boldness, loyalty, persuasiveness, and courage.

The pros and cons of having the gift of prophecy are listed below:

PROS	CONS
Studies and knows the scriptures	Overreacts at times to different situations
Reveals evil motives	Becomes too aggressive
Defends the truth	Knows he is targeted constantly by Satan
Confronts evil	Operates outside of the Holy Spirit if not careful

What to observe:

If this is your gift and you do not guard it, you may overreact to situations. Peter is a good example here. When Judas brought the soldiers to capture Jesus in the garden of Gethsemane, Peter, as the hot-tempered character we know him to be, responded by cutting off the ear of one of the soldiers. Imagine being in the presence of God, the Son, and thinking that Jesus needed someone to protect Him. Jesus restored the man's ear and thus demonstrates another lesson to Peter. There is no reason to overreact or even react when we are in God's presence and ministering under His power and authority.

A prophet knows he will be confronted with

false doctrine. That comes with the territory. In order to refute sin, it makes sense that his character would include being aggressive. Aggressive behavior means being ready or likely to confront a certain situation. When this behavior is called for, it is right. However, when it is an automatic response without thought or consideration, then it is not right. It's similar to jumping ahead of God. When we don't wait on God, we normally delay something He already has in play.

Of all the gifts, the gift of prophecy is the one that has the fewest number of people called to it. Those with this gift know that Satan will challenge them physically and emotionally; and he will challenge them through their families and service to God. Samuel was a prophet, judge, priest, and counselor who listened to God. And despite all the great things he is known for, we know his sons did not follow in his footsteps. As we can see in families today, we need continued prayer for God's protection.

When prophets operate outside of the Holy Spirit, pride steps in and creates a break in the relationship and the glory that is due to God. If Joseph had succumbed to the seduction of Potiphar's wife, what a tragedy that would have been to his legacy, after overcoming so much. He overcame being thrown into the pit by his brothers, being falsely accused, being thrown into prison twice, and more. You will see in the Genesis account, "but God was with Joseph." Joseph stayed true to God, even when he was being tested, time and time again. He was operating under the Holy Spirit.

Where to serve:
The person with this spiritual gift should find joy and be effective in serving in the following and similar types of ministries: Small Group, Lay Counseling, Communications, or Mentoring.

CHAPTER 4

THE GIFT OF SERVING

Serving is a spiritual gift that many people in the Kingdom of God have. It may not be their primary gift, but it is a gift of high importance within the church family. It is even said that some people do not think of it as a gift because they just like to help wherever they are needed.

Nevertheless, service is a spiritual gift.

According to The New Unger's Bible Dictionary, service is rendering work or attending to the needs of others.

A few scriptures in the Bible that refer to serving are listed below. You should study them more if you think this may be your gift.

Romans 12:1-2 MSG

So here's what I want you to do, God helping you: Take your everyday, ordinary life—your sleeping, eating, going-to-work, and walking-around life—and place it before God as an offering. Embracing what God does for you is the best thing you can do for him. Don't become so well-adjusted to your culture that you fit into it without even thinking. Instead, fix your attention on God. You'll be changed from the inside out. Readily recognize what he wants from you, and quickly respond to it. Unlike the culture around you, always dragging you down to its level of immaturity, God brings the best out of you, develops well-formed maturity in you.

Matthew 23:11-12 MSG

Do you want to stand out? Then step down. Be a servant. If you puff yourself up, you'll get the wind knocked out of you. But if you're content to simply be yourself, your life will count for plenty.

Joshua 22:5 MSG

Only this: Be vigilant in keeping the Commandment and The Revelation that Moses the servant of GOD laid on you: Love GOD, your God, walk in all his ways, do what he's commanded, embrace him, serve him with everything you are and have."

How do you know if you have the gift of serving? When you hear of a need, your mind immediately goes to the practical area to help the person in need. You cannot wait to offer them your assistance and support and, most of the time, it has something to do with using your hands. Your offer is sincere and cheerful. You may not even wait to be asked what you would like to do, instead you let them know multiple ways you are willing to help, assist, and support.

The person with this gift can also anticipate what needs to be done and will do it even before others realize it needs to be done.

Many people may like to serve, but those with this gift of service have a passion and desire to help that will not allow them to rest until the task is completed. People with this gift realize that others do not have this gift and, when those people try to help, they may end up being in the way or even significantly slowing down the process. You get it, that serving others is a way to be of service to God.

Think of people you know who serve and then think of those you observe who have this gift. People who serve with their hands can really make a difference in the execution of a specific ministry. Those who maintain the operation of church equipment, beautification of the church internally and externally, culinary skills to feed God's people for homeless or celebratory events are those who love to serve.

Most people with this gift serve with their heart even before they serve with their hands. For example, Mother Theresa comes to mind. She sacrificed her life to give of service to God by showing God's love to others. For her, others were, primarily, the poor and disadvantaged. She established centers in India for Lepers and a Hospice Center for people to die with dignity.

Mother Theresa is quoted as saying, "I am not sure exactly what heaven will be like, but I know that when we die and it comes time for God to judge us, he will not ask, 'How many good things have you done in your life?' rather he will ask, 'How much love did you put into what you did?'"

So, it is easy to see that an important part of being a server is having the right attitude. We should all be trying to be more like Christ, especially when we are serving, we want to demonstrate the right attitude for believers and non-believers to see.

If your attitude does not line up with your passion for service, it will quickly become evident. God gifted servers who want the serving environment to be a blessing to the ministry as well as to those being served.

Ask God, through prayer and meditation, to confirm if this is your gift.

Some of the people in the Bible with this gift were Timothy, the Good Samaritan, the Priests, Martha, and Ruth.

Timothy. We know from Paul's writings that Timothy was a young protégé of his. We are told early on that Timothy was raised by a devoted believing mother, Eunice and grandmother, Lois. Paul sent Timothy to Ephesus to lead this church. He encouraged him not to be timid because he was young. He was encouraged to be confident of his calling and to follow the Holy Spirit in leading the church.

The Good Samaritan. The story of the Good Samaritan is one of the more well-known stories in the Bible. There are so many lessons you can learn from the Good Samaritan. We can all fall upon hard times, whether physical, spiritual, financial, or emotional. In those times, we need someone to help us, serve us, come beside us, and support us until we can get back on our feet. Those whom we may expect to help us may not. But those with the heart for serving will not be able to walk away without doing something to help.

Luke 10:25-37 MSG

25 Just then a religion scholar stood up with a question to test Jesus. "Teacher, what do I need to do to get eternal life?"
26 He answered, "What's written in God's Law? How do you interpret it?"
27 He said, "That you love the Lord your God with all your passion and prayer and muscle and intelligence—and that you love your neighbor as well as you do yourself."
28 "Good answer!" said Jesus. "Do it and you'll live."
29 Looking for a loophole, he asked, "And just how would you define 'neighbor'?"

30-32 Jesus answered by telling a story. "There was once a man traveling from Jerusalem to Jericho. On the way he was attacked by robbers. They took his clothes, beat him up, and went off leaving him half-dead. Luckily, a priest was on his way down the same road, but when he saw him he angled across to the other side. Then a Levite religious man showed up; he also avoided the injured man.

33-35 "A Samaritan traveling the road came on him. When he saw the man's condition, his heart went out to him. He gave him first aid, disinfecting and bandaging his wounds. Then he lifted him onto his donkey, led him to an inn, and made him comfortable. In the morning he took out two silver coins and gave them to the innkeeper, saying, 'Take good care of him. If it costs any more, put it on my bill—I'll pay you on my way back.'

36 "What do you think? Which of the three became a neighbor to the man attacked by robbers?"

37 "The one who treated him kindly," the religion scholar responded.

Jesus said, "Go and do the same."

Priests. The priests were descendants of Levi and called to be servants of God. They had the special anointing to sacrifice the animals, to bless the people to God, and to carry the ark of the covenant. You will see priests and Levites written together in certain scriptures. As it was said in several resources, all priests are Levites, but not all Levites are priests. It could be described as: priests were responsible for the holier services. Levites served the upkeep of the tabernacle and served the priests.

<u>Martha.</u> The story of Mary and Martha is found in the Gospels. It is not only a well-known story of two women, but there are songs, poems, and art dedicated to this story and about this account in the Bible. When Jesus visited His friends, Mary, Martha and Lazarus; Martha was busy serving while Mary sat at Jesus' feet to learn from Him. Martha's gift may have been serving, but the lesson to be drawn from this story is choosing the best over the good.

Luke 10:38-42 MSG

38-40 As they continued their travel, Jesus entered a village. A woman by the name of Martha welcomed him and made him feel quite at home. She had a sister, Mary, who sat before the Master, hanging on every word he said. But Martha was pulled away by all she had to do in the kitchen. Later, she stepped in, interrupting them. "Master, don't you care that my sister has abandoned the kitchen to me? Tell her to lend me a hand."

41-42 The Master said, "Martha, dear Martha, you're fussing far too much and getting yourself worked up over nothing. One thing only is essential, and Mary has chosen it—it's the main course, and won't be taken from her."

Ruth. You rarely hear the name Ruth without the name Naomi. In order to save his family from the famine in Bethlehem, Elimelech took his wife, Naomi, and two sons to Moab, a distance of more than 1800 miles. Elimelech died sometime later and their sons married two Moabite women. Ten years later the two sons died. Naomi decided to return to Bethlehem. One daughter-in-law returned to her family and the other daughter-in-law, Ruth, stayed with and served Naomi. Naomi's advice to Ruth resulted in a marriage to Boaz. This places Ruth in Jesus' lineage.

The characteristics of those with this gift are caring, faithful, loyal, energetic, hospitable, and gracious.

The pros and cons of having the gift of serving are listed below:

PROS	CONS
Hears the Word and does what the Word says	Gets involved in too many projects
Enjoys short term projects	Forgets spiritual side of serving sometimes
Completes tasks on time	Acts too quickly at times
Feels excitement to get the job done	Does most of the work and leaves little work for others

What to observe:

Getting involved in too many projects is one of the first things we learn in reading Exodus 18. Moses is overwhelmed and under stress as he is trying to hear all the disputes arising during the Israelites' journey in the wilderness. (According to the Bible there were more than 600,000 Israelite men when they left Egypt.) If we are involved in too many projects or too much of one project, it will eventually impact our effectiveness and our health. Knowing when to stop, assess the situation, and get the right help will make us more efficient where we should be. In this chapter, Jethro, Moses' father-in-law, gave him timeless advice, to get help.

Serving primarily has a physical side, but it also has a spiritual side. During the Thanksgiving holidays especially, we hear about many churches and non-profits serving dinner to the disadvantaged. While this is truly a noble undertaking, we must always be sensitive to the reason we are serving. We are not serving so our church or organization can receive news coverage, so that we can show that we have the money to do it, but that we are being obedient to God. We want to please God.

Serving in the Holy Spirit means we have heard what and how our service will benefit those who are served and give glory to God. If we respond too quickly, we may not consider the best way to make a difference in the long term. An old Chinese proverb is debated as being the first to state, "Give a man a fish, he eats for a day; if you teach a man to fish, he eats for a lifetime." So, in planning, the first meal is a quick fix but putting a plan together for a more permanent fix is better in the long-term.

We are all a part of God's body. As such, the other parts can play a significant role in the serving. Some give expertise, some give money, some give their hands for service and so forth. If we make decisions in isolation, we sometimes leave little for others to do. Working in concert with others, gives God pleasure and gives us a good feeling that we have shared in serving those considered as the least of these (Mat. 25:40). We can truly celebrate together when we have all contributed to something of value, whether tangible or intangible.

Where to serve:
The person with this gift will find joy and be effective in the following and similar types of ministries: Deacons, Hospitality, Children/Youth, Homeless, Property Management, Benevolence, Culinary and Floral.

CHAPTER 5

THE GIFT OF TEACHING

When we think of teaching, we think of a person giving instruction in some academic discipline. We know that all the gifts are important because we need all the gifts functioning cohesively to make a church operate effectively. The gift of teaching is important to ensure that the truth is being taught and that we are guiding and inspiring the next generation into the service of the Kingdom.

The New Unger's Bible Dictionary states that "inasmuch as men are delivered from the bondage of sin and build up in righteousness through the agency of truth, teaching becomes essential."

How will you know if teaching is your spiritual gift? You will have an extreme desire to know the Word, understand the Word, and share the Word.

This is my primary gift, and I can't tell you how excited and thankful I was when God confirmed this to me. I found myself reading and studying and preparing way into the wee hours of the morning. One scripture would lead to another, then another until my eyes were tired from reading, and my hand hurt from writing. At times, I had an overabundance of materials and interesting facts to share with my students. Engaging them with the stories, maps, charts, and application to today's issues was my primary goal.

Are you ignoring your gift? Initially, I ignored my gift. I came from a long line of teachers so instead of pursuing a degree in Education, I chose Accounting. I did not find the joy and enthusiasm that I found when I realized my gift was in teaching. Finding your gift will be an ever-pursuing thirst for more of whatever that gift is. You will stay up day and night to pursue the excellence you want to demonstrate when you execute your gift. I ask you again, are you ignoring your gift?

Somewhere, I read an article on how to identify your passion, which leads you to your spiritual gift. The question to ask yourself is, what would you do if money nor time was an object? Another question to ask is, what problem would you address if money and time were not a concern?

A few scriptures in the Bible that refer to teaching are listed below. You should study them and others if you think this may be your gift.

Psalm 32:8-9 CSB

⁸ I will instruct you and show you the way to go;
with my eye on you, I will give counsel.
⁹ Do not be like a horse or mule,
without understanding,
that must be controlled with bit and bridle
or else it will not come near you.

Colossians 1:28-29 CSB

²⁸ We proclaim him, warning and teaching everyone with all wisdom, so that we may present everyone mature in Christ.

²⁹ I labor for this, striving with his strength that works powerfully in me.

Matthew 5:1-12 CSB

When he saw the crowds, he went up on the mountain, and after he sat down, his disciples came to him.

² Then[a] he began to teach them, saying:

The Beatitudes

³ "Blessed are the poor in spirit,
for the kingdom of heaven is theirs.
⁴ Blessed are those who mourn,
for they will be comforted.
⁵ Blessed are the humble,
for they will inherit the earth.

6 Blessed are those who hunger and thirst for
righteousness,
for they will be filled.
7 Blessed are the merciful,
for they will be shown mercy.
8 Blessed are the pure in heart,
for they will see God.
9 Blessed are the peacemakers,
for they will be called sons of God.
10 Blessed are those who are persecuted because of
righteousness,
for the kingdom of heaven is theirs.

11 "You are blessed when they insult you and persecute you
and falsely say every kind of evil against you because of
me.

12 Be glad and rejoice, because your reward is great in
heaven. For that is how they persecuted the prophets who
were before you.

Matthew 28:18-20 CSB

18 Jesus came near and said to them, "All authority has
been given to me in heaven and on earth.
19 Go, therefore, and make disciples of[e] all
nations, baptizing them in the name of the Father and of the
Son and of the Holy Spirit,
20 teaching them to observe everything I have commanded
you. And remember,[f] I am with you always,[g] to the end of
the age."

Think back to your school days. Who was your favorite teacher? What teacher inspired or encouraged you to enter your current field or industry? What did you like about them back then? What do you appreciate about them today? It is such a sad commentary on the compensation that teachers are paid in many countries. Many teachers look at their careers as a calling just as we expect a pastor to be called.

As stated earlier, those with the gift of teaching have a desire to know the truth and share the truth. They will take inordinate amounts of time to confirm what is true and present it in a way that produces "aha" moments out of their students.

Think again about your favorite teacher. What method did they use to pique your interest? It's as if they did not stop until they could see the glimmer in your eye confirming that you understood the concept. That is what brings joy to a teacher, knowing that the student "got it" is priceless to a teacher.

As we know, all parents and guardians are teachers whether they are good or not so good. Sometimes, the child or the students learn the lessons later rather than sooner.

For Biblical lessons, God encourages teachers to continue teaching by ensuring us that if we complete our part and He will do the rest.

The Bible warns all believers not to think too highly of themselves. This is a concern for those who teach. Teachers can be enthusiastic to share the truth of God, but teachers should not gloat because they are knowledgeable. That could make other learners feel uncomfortable to participate in a discussion, where all could learn more.

Persons in the Bible with this gift were Luke, Gamaliel, Priscilla and Aquila, and Apollos.

Luke. Known as the Gentile Physician, he who created an orderly historical account of Jesus' birth and life. He was a loyal companion traveling with Paul and ministering to him and others that were sick or hurt. His Gospel is the longest and most encompassing of the others. He is also attributed to writing the book of Acts. He was well-educated which supports his ability to write for the purpose of telling the specific details that teach us more than any other Gospels.

Gamaliel. Gamaliel was a Pharisee, scholar, teacher, and doctor of the law. His short account is in Acts 5:33-40 NKJV. He was the grandson of Hillel, also known for his wisdom. At a time when the apostles were brought before the Sanhedrin

Council for fervency in preaching to grow the church, Gamaliel used his reputation to save them. He reckoned with the Council: "Men of Israel, take heed to yourselves what you intend to do regarding these men....

And now I say to you, keep away from these men and let them alone; for if this plan or this work is of men, it will come to nothing; but if it is of God, you cannot overthrow it – lest you even be found to fight against God." It should be noted that Saul/Paul was a student of Gamaliel.

Priscilla and Aquila. This wife and husband team are always mentioned together in the Bible. They left Rome when Claudius expelled the Jews and went to Corinth. There they met Paul who lived with them for more than a year, as tentmakers. Sitting under Paul's teachings, they were converted. They accompanied Paul to Ephesus and later returned to Rome, where their home was a place for Christians to gather and learn about Jesus.

Apollos. He is also known as a student of the scriptures and a great speaker. In Acts 18:24-28, we learn that he went to Ephesus to preach. He had not heard that the Messiah had come, so his teaching was incomplete. Basically, he was an eloquent speaker, but his knowledge was about Christianity up to the time of John the Baptist.

When Priscilla and Aquila heard his zeal for the Word without the details about the Messiah, they took him aside and shared the full Gospel with Apollos. He accepted the teachings and went forth spreading the Word with even more power. He left Ephesus and preached in Achaia and Corinth.

The characteristics of those with this gift are studious, inspiring, creative, intelligent detailed-oriented, caring, and energetic.

The pros and cons of having the gift of teaching are listed below:

PROS	CONS
Uses systematic learning	Maintains traditional learning styles
Finds precise answers	Can be long-winded
Researches different sources for answers	Demonstrates prideful behavior at times
Checking facts from different sources	Becomes frustrated with slow/moderate learners

What to observe:
Times have changed so it's important to change with the times. As educators, teachers want to see that their students understand the topic or the concept. If there is a faster, better way for the student to comprehend, teachers should be eager to use those methods and not resist them. Ray T.

Bernard is quoted as saying, "It's only after you've stepped outside your comfort zone that you begin to change, grow, and transform." Successful teachers must be willing to change from older methods of learning to newer methods that engage new and younger students.

Best practices represent the most effective ways to complete a set of procedures. Whether it's teaching, learning, studying, memorizing, or other activities, time will always play a part. So it is with the teacher. If you are too talkative, the students may miss the point or totally lose interest. In planning for each segment of your lesson, determine an adequate amount of time for each subtopic. As you go along, you can still be flexible to continue or stop earlier based on their level of understanding, interest, and engagement.

No one likes to feel like they are ignorant of something they should know. Yet some teachers may think too highly of their own education and unintentionally make others feel too uncomfortable to participate. If a teacher continuously creates this type of environment, it will become more of a lecture style than interactive discussions which stimulate better understanding.

Who said patience is a virtue? William Langland quoted this expression in his poem, Piers Plowman in the 14th century. Per Wikipedia, "…the speaker experiences seven steps on his quest to live a good Christian life." Understanding patience in the right context is most important. Patience is a virtue when God has commanded us to wait. So in our teaching, if we are called to repeat, explain, expand, or give multiple examples to help a student learn, then why not be patient for them to "get it". We should do this in love, to those who may need a little extra encouragement. Not every subject is easy for everyone. Let's use patience when we teach God's Word.

Where to serve:
The person with this gift will find joy and be effective in the following and similar types of ministries: Bible Study, Sunday School, Vacation Bible School, and Bible Institutes.

CHAPTER 6

THE GIFT OF EXHORTATION

How will you know if you have the gift of exhortation? You are a caring person who does not want to see people go to hell. This gift is a job crucial to the body of Christ. You want to warn people of the detrimental consequences of their actions. You feel the need to warn people that they are sinners, that they were born in sin, and that they cannot stop sinning on their own.

People with this gift come with a sort of one-two punch. First, the exhorter warns the people, then shares the Good News, that they can avoid their current path to destruction. God knew that we would be unable to avoid the path on our own. He knew this from the beginning with Adam and Eve. And that is why He provided a way of escape.

A few scriptures in the Bible that refer to exhortation are listed below. You should study them more if you think this may be your gift.

I Thessalonians 2:3-5 KJV

3 For our exhortation was not of deceit, nor of uncleanness, nor in guile:

⁴ But as we were allowed of God to be put in trust with the gospel, even so we speak; not as pleasing men, but God, which trieth our hearts.
⁵ For neither at any time used we flattering words, as ye know, nor a cloke of covetousness; God is witness:

Acts 14:21-23 KJV

²¹ And when they had preached the gospel to that city, and had taught many, they returned to Lystra, and to Iconium, and Antioch,
²² Confirming the souls of the disciples, and exhorting them to continue in the faith, and that we must through much tribulation enter into the kingdom of God.
²³ And when they had ordained them elders in every church, and had prayed with fasting, they commended them to the Lord, on whom they believed.

Hebrews 10:19-25 KJV

¹⁹ Having therefore, brethren, boldness to enter into the holiest by the blood of Jesus,
²⁰ By a new and living way, which he hath consecrated for us, through the veil, that is to say, his flesh;
²¹ And having an high priest over the house of God;
²² Let us draw near with a true heart in full assurance of faith, having our hearts sprinkled from an evil conscience, and our bodies washed with pure water.
²³ Let us hold fast the profession of our faith without wavering; (for he is faithful that promised;)
²⁴ And let us consider one another to provoke unto love and to good works:
²⁵ Not forsaking the assembling of ourselves together, as the manner of some is; but exhorting one another: and so much the more, as ye see the day approaching.

This is a great gift to be anointed with because this person can start out sharing about a bad place in the present but end up in the best place for the future.

We have all had an exhorter in our lives. How did they help you see the light? It may have started with a pastor, but more than likely you have had others speak up in critical times during your life's journey.

The exhorter may have approached you in a fiery delivery so they could get your attention. You knew the exhorter was sent from God. This is where fear is a positive. When a person realizes that they are in a physical fire, they know it is time to escape. So it is when a person finally realizes that they are on a fiery path to spiritual destruction, they are then ready to follow a path of escape.

Most of us began feeling the heat and that is what pushed us to decide. An exhorter has experienced the same type of high heat, so they know the danger signs. They do not want you to continue down this path. They want you to get off the train that is headed off the cliff.

Now, they finally have your attention! The exhorter enjoys the relief that comes with Part II. However, sometimes the encouraging part can come first. Say, for example, an unbelieving friend comes to you complaining about a certain situation. Let's say that they are angry with their spouse. In this situation, you can encourage them to try all they can to make the marriage work, but then warn them that God created marriage and when God is not in the marriage, it is doomed for serious problems and/or failure. Why wouldn't the created seek the advice of the Creator? Just as a person wanting to repair a refrigerator without seeking the advice of the manufacturer. Does that make sense? Warning them that Satan is roving the earth looking for who he can "steal, kill and destroy".

I Peter 5:8-11 KJV

8 Be sober, be vigilant; because your adversary the devil, as a roaring lion, walketh about, seeking whom he may devour:
9 Whom resist stedfast in the faith, knowing that the same afflictions are accomplished in your brethren that are in the world.
10 But the God of all grace, who hath called us unto his eternal glory by Christ Jesus, after that ye have suffered a while, make you perfect, stablish, strengthen, settle you.
11 To him be glory and dominion for ever and ever. Amen.

The person with the gift of exhortation will be alert to these opportunities and steer the conversation to repentance and peace. The exhorter knows that peace, from the turmoil in their life, is what their friend is searching for. Right now, they are in the heat of things and in pain. But fear not, God has provided a way out and the exhorter is there to show them the way.

Persons in the Bible with this gift include Paul, Noah, Elisha, and the Woman at the Well.

Paul. Paul, born Saul, is the writer of two-thirds of the New Testament. As Saul, he was a scholar and a zealous persecutor of Christians. He received permission from the high priest to pursue the Christians, persecute and imprison men and women, and even vote for their deaths. While on a journey to seek Christians in Damascus, Paul was converted. His conversion was immediate yet complete. From that time forth he was sent to the Gentiles to warn them of the truth of the Gospel and to encourage them to accept the Jesus he had persecuted.

Noah. Noah is an Old Testament figure that is associated with building the ark. The Bible story tells that men were so evil God decided to destroy all the people of the earth. Even after making this decision, various accounts state that God allowed 120 years to pass. Noah was around 480 years old when he was assigned the task of warning the people to repent as he builds the ark based on God's specifications. His warning was simple, but it was ignored. He was 600 years old and the flood came. All were lost except Noah, his family and two of each kind of animal and fowl. God shut the door of the ark Himself.

Elisha. A story of warning in the Bible takes place in the book of 2 Kings 6:8-23. God would tell Elisha when to warn the King of Israel about the King of Aram's plans to attack. It happened so often that King Aram thought there was a spy in his own camp. When he was told that God was giving the word to Elisha for the king, he ordered his troops to capture Elisha. And when the Arameans attempted to capture Elisha, God blinded their eyes and then led them from Dothan to Samaria. Instead of killing them in Samaria, God opened their eyes. When the King of Israel saw them, instead of killing them, Elisha informed the king to feed them and send them home.

The Woman at the Well. Most church goers have heard the story of the Woman at the Well. It is the story of a Samaritan woman going to the well during the heat of the day to avoid others. When she arrives, Jesus was alone and asks her for a drink. Ordinarily, Samaritans and Jews kept separate from each other. That conversation led to Jesus telling her about her adulterous lifestyle and how He was offering her living water. She accepted and was converted. She, then, went to the neighboring town and implored them, encouraged them to come see a man who told her all about her life. Many came to see Jesus and accepted Him as their Savior, too.

The characteristics of a person with this gift will be honesty, self-confidence, intelligence, seriousness, helpfulness, and care.

The pros and cons of having the gift of exhortation are listed below:

PROS	CONS
Cares sincerely for people	Becomes overzealous at times
Encourages spiritual growth	Works too intently
Explains God's purpose	Exhibits aggressiveness
Displays selflessness	Expresses an uncaring nature periodically

What to observe:
Do you find yourself excited to share good news with those you love? That can be a good thing if they are at a similar place in their lives. If not, they may reject what you want to share and consider you overzealous in trying to control their spiritual walk. Knowing that the latter could be the case, I encourage you to plan what you want to share. For example, you may be excited when you first

confirm your spiritual gifts. Now that you know yours, you think everybody should want to know theirs. You will soon find out that some will, and some won't. Let that not discourage you from your own excitement. Pray for the day the other person discovers their spiritual gifts.

Excess in most things can cause a problem in some area of your life. We know that Peter had an intense personality, but we can surmise that he learned his lesson when he wrote 1 Peter 2:11. According to the Message Translation, he explains that we should not indulge our ego at the expense of our soul. When we work too intently, it is normally to fulfill some personal objective. We want to minister in a way that pleases God. Being acknowledged by others could be a product of our ministry, but that should not be the purpose.

As I mentioned previously, aggression means ready or likely to attack or confront a thing. When we remember how Saul was before his conversion on the road to Damascus, we can understand how that behavior could carry over from his old ways into his new ministry. As Saul, we know that he believed he was doing what was right, to persecute Christians and have them imprisoned as a way to protect Judaism. That aggressiveness to confront others was redirected when he met Jesus Christ and became Paul.

As exhorters and encouragers, we cannot afford to be viewed as uncaring. If we think our ministry is all about us and not about Jesus and others, we may inadvertently portray an uncaring spirit. It's not about us and it's all to please Jesus...to share the Good News with the unsaved. If the exhorter's secondary gift is serving, giving, or mercy that will help in displaying a caring spirit.

Where to serve:
The person with this gift will find joy and effectiveness in the following and similar types of ministries: Missions, Evangelism, Outreach, Counseling, and Music and Arts.

CHAPTER 7

THE GIFT OF GIVING

How will you know if your spiritual gift is giving? As soon as you hear of a need, you cannot wait to offer money, resources, or time to alleviate the need. "How can I help?" "What do they need?" "Here is $2,000. Just let me know how much more you will need."

These are the questions and statements that you will hear from people with this gift. One of the reasons they can jump to give is because they have the resources and funds. They have the resources and funds because they have been good stewards over what money and property they have earned or received.

To give means to make a present of, to bestow a donation. It can be a donation of treasure, time, and talent.

A few scriptures in the Bible that refer to giving are listed below. You should study them and more if you think this may be your gift.

2 Corinthians 9:6-10 NLT

⁶ *Remember this—a farmer who plants only a few seeds will get a small crop. But the one who plants generously will get a generous crop.*
⁷ *You must each decide in your heart how much to give. And don't give reluctantly or in response to pressure. "For God loves a person who gives cheerfully."*[c]
⁸ *And God will generously provide all you need. Then you will always have everything you need and plenty left over to share with others.*
⁹ *As the Scriptures say,*
"They share freely and give generously to the poor.
Their good deeds will be remembered forever."[d]
¹⁰ *For God is the one who provides seed for the farmer and then bread to eat. In the same way, he will provide and increase your resources and then produce a great harvest of generosity*[e] *in you.*

Deuteronomy 15:7-11 NLT

⁷ *"But if there are any poor Israelites in your towns when you arrive in the land the LORD your God is giving you, do not be hard-hearted or tightfisted toward them.*
⁸ *Instead, be generous and lend them whatever they need.*
⁹ *Do not be mean-spirited and refuse someone a loan because the year for canceling debts is close at hand. If you refuse to make the loan and the needy person cries out to the LORD, you will be considered guilty of sin.*
¹⁰ *Give generously to the poor, not grudgingly, for the LORD your God will bless you in everything you do.*
¹¹ *There will always be some in the land who are poor. That is why I am commanding you to share freely with the poor and with other Israelites in need.*

2 Corinthians 8:3-7 NLT

3 For I can testify that they gave not only what they could afford, but far more. And they did it of their own free will.
4 They begged us again and again for the privilege of sharing in the gift for the believers in Jerusalem.[b]
5 They even did more than we had hoped, for their first action was to give themselves to the Lord and to us, just as God wanted them to do.
6 So we have urged Titus, who encouraged your giving in the first place, to return to you and encourage you to finish this ministry of giving.
7 Since you excel in so many ways—in your faith, your gifted speakers, your knowledge, your enthusiasm, and your love from us[c]—I want you to excel also in this gracious act of giving.

Malachi 3:8-10 NLT

8 "Should people cheat God? Yet you have cheated me! "But you ask, 'What do you mean? When did we ever cheat you?'
"You have cheated me of the tithes and offerings due to me.
9 You are under a curse, for your whole nation has been cheating me.
10 Bring all the tithes into the storehouse so there will be enough food in my Temple. If you do," says the LORD of Heaven's Armies, "I will open the windows of heaven for you. I will pour out a blessing so great you won't have enough room to take it in! Try it! Put me to the test!

The people with this gift know for certain the value of money and how it can be used to give

God glory. Many people with this gift like to give anonymously. They are not looking for recognition for what they give.

If people with this gift have acquired the wealth from hard work and meager beginnings, they are more cognizant of what it feels like to be in a state of lack. If they realize the sacrifice their families endured to acquire an inheritance, they may also feel the need to give back as others shared with them in their time of need.

On the other hand, these people could also step up to lead a special fundraising project. They realize that lending their name or reputation for the financial success of a cause will motivate others to give.

According to Wikipedia, GoFundMe is an online for-profit way to raise money for many different causes. From 2010-2017, $5 million was raised by fifty million donors. This makes it easier for everyone to give to something they may be passionate about. Having a famous philanthropist or institution endorse the cause can be invaluable to the charity or event.

A person with this gift will not limit themselves to the 10% tithe way of thinking. This person will give far above 10% and may give money, property, time, energy, and talent multiple times during a fundraising campaign. Hearing of a shortfall in the promoted goal, a person with this gift will rise to the occasion to top off the giving. According to Forbes Magazine, the top known 50 givers in the United States are also a part of the Forbes top 400 companies.

These same people may offer access to buildings or property that they own, or they may allow their employees time off to mentor, repair, clean, etc. in support of the disadvantaged. Many entertainers who recognize their talents are from God, will host a concert and donate the proceeds to charitable causes.

Big Brothers and Big Sisters' mission is to "provide a caring adult mentor to every child that needs one." These caring adults are donating their time to make a difference in the life of a youth who needs someone to listen to them and talk with them.

Persons and situations in the Bible that express a spirit of giving are Matthew, the Woman with the Alabaster Box, the Widow's Two Mites, and the Roman Centurion.

Matthew. The Gospel of Matthew has more references to giving than all the others. Because Matthew, also known as Levi, was a tax collector, he was most familiar with financial transactions.

God called him right from his place and occupation of collecting taxes from the Jews for the Roman government. It was a hated profession. When he was converted, he gave a big reception for Jesus and invited other tax collectors as guests. He lived in Capernaum and eventually preached for more than 10 years in Judea after Jesus' ascension.

The Woman with the Alabaster Box. This story is found in Matthew 26:6-13; Mark 14:3-9, and John 12:1-11. Jesus was at the home of a leper when this unnamed woman (probably Martha and Lazarus' sister, Mary) comes in and proceeds to pour the ointment from the alabaster box on the head of Jesus (John indicates she anointed his feet). The value of the perfume is compared to one year's wages of a laborer. The point here is her devotion to Jesus and her desire to give Him something of great value.

The Widow's Two Mites. In Luke 21:1-4 and Mark 12:41-44, Jesus observes as people place their offerings in the treasury. He sees the rich but also sees a widow who only had two mites to give. Two mites were the equivalent of one cent, yet Jesus said she gave more than the rich. The rich gave out of their abundance and would not miss it, but she gave out of her poverty and would.

The Roman Centurion. This is a most unusual story about giving. In the scriptures, it says that the Roman Centurion had faith enough in Jesus to ask Him to heal his servant. He did not go to Jesus himself, but sent elders of the Jews to ask on his behalf. The elders were willing to go because the Roman Centurion had demonstrated his love for the nation of Israel by giving toward the building of a synagogue. What a great story about giving in that one ethnic group gave a large enough donation to another ethnic group to build them a place of worship.

Characteristics of people with this gift are generous, thoughtful, caring, wise with money, resourceful, and thankful.

The pros and cons of having the gift of giving are listed below:

PROS	CONS
Gives time, talent, their name as well as money	Ignores pressure of others to give
Desires to give sincerely	Condemns non-givers or lesser givers
Demonstrates prudence in giving	Forgets the spiritual part of giving
Donates anonymously at times	Controls the project because they are the largest giver

What to observe:
Fundraising can be a time of anxiety for church leaders because they have determined a need and now they must trust God to lead them through the process of fulfilling it. If there are many roadblocks, the congregation may challenge whether or not the leaders heard from God. Is the project to elevate the leader's ego or to erect a facility to expand the church's outreach ministry? Givers may want to give, when and how much they want to give regardless of the pressure of the leaders.

Givers may condemn non-givers which can be dangerous because they do not have all the facts of who has already given. Sometimes non-givers are responsible for large third-party endowments. The perceived non-givers may have given in-kind donations or promised future contributions. In the end, the givers can only know their own intent and contribution amount. Ultimately, we should each be concerned with our own giving. Speaking out about perceived non-givers can create an uncomfortable environment.

It just so happens that, at this time, I am receiving a teaching on "The Blessed Life" by Robert Morris. The subtitle is *Unlocking the Reward of Generous Living*. He laid out in the first chapter that God is the reason we are to give. He gave us the best example of giving when He gave His son. When givers have the resources to give, it is a form of acknowledgement that God has given to them and that they know God desires them to give to others. We are being obedient when we understand it is a blessing to have and a blessing to give.

If the giver wants to control the project because they are the major donor, there is a problem of the heart. Just as the church is made up of many parts, so will the project involve many parts. You will need the expertise of various partners to execute the project. The person with the gift of Administration should coordinate with those with the different skills to effectively lead the project to a timely completion. One person should not control the project just because they are the largest donor.

Where to serve:
The person with this gift finds effectiveness and joy in the following and similar types of ministries: Stewards, Property Management, Outreach, Benevolence, and Scholarship.

CHAPTER 8

THE GIFT OF ADMINISTRATION

How will you know if you have the gift of administration? You get nervous or agitated when you see disorder, or when there seems to be no leader. Is the current leader being wishy-washy? Is the leader inconsiderate of others' abilities? Do they downplay others' ideas?

If these statements and questions come to mind, then this is probably your spiritual gift. It is also called the Gift of Leadership or Organization.

A leader guides, directs, commands, manages, and goes first to represent the organization.

There can be many levels of leadership in a church. Within the Baptist church, which is how I grew up, there is the senior pastor who is the overall administrator. In some other denominations, the top administrator is called the Overseer. Then, there could be multiple assistant pastors, associate pastors, ministers, ministry leaders, assistant ministry leaders, and special committee chairmen/chairwomen.

I think you would be hard pressed to find that each one of these positions is filled with those with the predominant gift of administration. At the printing of this book, many mega churches with multiple campuses post their organizational chart which reflects the positions and the responsible officers to make the operation work, similar to large for-profit corporations.

The concern arises when the senior pastor's spiritual gift is prophecy or proclaiming and/or teaching; and must lead the church in its organization and its operation. What can be done to utilize others in his inner circle with the gift of administration and maintain unity, peace, and effectiveness throughout the other ministries? Some forward-thinking churches are now allowing the senior pastors to focus on the preaching and pastoring while allowing assistant and associate pastors to serve as executive pastors and pastors of administration.

This is relatively new and, as you would imagine, it will not work for every church for different reasons. As with everything, the leadership team will need to go deep into prayer to see what will work for their individual church.

A few scriptures in the Bible that refer to administration are listed below. You should study them and others if you think this may be your gift.

James 1:22-24 MSG

22-24 Don't fool yourself into thinking that you are a listener when you are anything but, letting the Word go in one ear and out the other. Act on what you hear! Those who hear and don't act are like those who glance in the mirror, walk away, and two minutes later have no idea who they are, what they look like.

Ephesians 1:20-23 MSG

20-23 All this energy issues from Christ: God raised him from death and set him on a throne in deep heaven, in charge of running the universe, everything from galaxies to governments, no name and no power exempt from his rule. And not just for the time being, but forever. He is in charge of it all, has the final word on everything. At the center of all this, Christ rules the church. The church, you see, is not peripheral to the world; the world is peripheral to the church. The church is Christ's body, in which he speaks and acts, by which he fills everything with his presence.

Isaiah 55:1-5 MSG

1-5 "Hey there! All who are thirsty,
 come to the water!
Are you penniless?
 Come anyway—buy and eat!
Come, buy your drinks, buy wine and milk.
 Buy without money—everything's free!
Why do you spend your money on junk food,
 your hard-earned cash on cotton candy?

Listen to me, listen well: Eat only the best,
  fill yourself with only the finest.
Pay attention, come close now,
  listen carefully to my life-giving, life-nourishing words.
I'm making a lasting covenant commitment with you,
  the same that I made with David: sure, solid, enduring
love.
I set him up as a witness to the nations,
  made him a prince and leader of the nations,
And now I'm doing it to you:
  You'll summon nations you've never heard of,
and nations who've never heard of you
  will come running to you
Because of me, your GOD,
  because The Holy of Israel has honored you."

The person with this gift knows what God wants and knows the detailed steps needed to get to the result. Although this person may or may not be a visionary, this person knows how to work with those who have the gift of prophecy and collaboratively work to execute the vision with timeliness and effectiveness.

If a new ministry is forming and there is no obvious or appointed leader, the person with this gift will step up to guide the start, formation, and general operating functions of this ministry.

If a ministry is already in existence, this person is gifted to assess whether the purpose, order, guidance, accountability, recordkeeping, and direction are aligned with the pastor. If they do not see an emerging new and better leader, they will be the one to volunteer and steer the ministry until a person with the appropriate leadership skills is appointed.

The absence of order and the potential for disorder totally frustrates a person with the gift of administration. If working in a secondary position, this person is constantly observing the skills of those around them to see who can bring stability and forward movement. 'Who should be next in line for the leadership position?' is their question.

The book *Lead Like Jesus* by Ken Blanchard and Phil Hodges should be required reading for a person who wants to confirm or expand their leadership gift. Jesus is the greatest example of all the gifts. Within the spiritual gift of leadership, Jesus of course, is the greatest leader. He knows how to communicate with His disciples/team. He knows when to ask questions, when to give commands, when to use parables, when to be direct, and all the things a great leader needs to do for success. Jesus also knows how and when to share information that will inspire His followers to learn the lessons He teaches.

People in the Bible demonstrating this gift of leadership are James (Jesus' brother), Moses, Gideon, and David.

James. James, the brother of Jesus, was considered a leader. Even though he was late to believe in Jesus, he was eventually converted and led the Jerusalem Counsel in their decision of how to treat the new Gentile believers. Some felt that Gentiles must be circumcised and follow other Jewish traditions in order to be saved. Each side presented their position and, afterwards, James judged that Gentiles would be accepted based on their faith and repentance but would not need to be circumcised. This was accepted by the Council and has been followed ever since.

Moses. Moses was chosen by God to lead the people out of Egypt and is well-known as the deliverer, lawgiver, and prophet. He was born during the decree for all newborn boys to be killed. His mother, Jochebed, was able to hide him for several months until she had to place him in the Nile River where he was found and raised by Pharaoh's daughter.

Growing up in the palace gave Moses preferences but when he realized the injustice to his people, he got in an altercation, murdered an Egyptian, and ran. When he returned, God spoke to him, saying that he would deliver his people from Egypt. This deliverance was accomplished after 10 plagues and the escape through the Red Sea. The journey through the wilderness took 40 years. Moses also received the 10 Commandments during this journey. However, he was not allowed to enter the Promised Land because of an act of disobedience.

Gideon. When we meet Gideon, he is in hiding and indicates no resemblance to the leader he would become. He is hiding in a winepress and threshing wheat. He wonders why God has forsaken his people, as they are currently impoverished and being taken advantage of by the Midianites. Gideon accepted the call to leadership but is known for requesting confirmation from God that it was God who was leading him.

Gideon's name was changed to Jerubbaal which means "Contender with Baal". Later his name was changed again to Jerubbesheth, which means "Contender with the Idol". It is presumed the last name change was to escape the reference to Baal. He went on to overthrow the Midianites with only the 300 men God required, after the famous Fleece test. Gideon eventually became a judge and led honorably for 40 years. His story is told in Judges, chapters 6-9.

David. The story of David is so interesting for a number of reasons, but one is the fact that he was chosen and anointed to be king privately as a youth but did not actually become king of Judah publicly until age 30. Later, he would be anointed king over Judah and Israel. In the interim, he experienced many opportunities where he demonstrated a command for leadership. He guided his sheep, he stepped up to fight the Philistine giant Goliath, he led armies against the Philistines, and he led his men when running from the current king, King Saul who had become jealous of David.

When he did take the kingship, he served for 40 years. He was a great administrator and was acknowledged for the genius of making Jerusalem the capital, which pleased the north and the south inhabitants. As a military master, he defeated the Philistines, Moabites, Aramaeans, Ammonites, Edomites, and Amalekites. His organizational skills of the kingdom itself are attributed to an Egyptian format, by creating different functions and different divisions. He formed Levitical Cities, Cities of Refuge, and made Jerusalem a religious center.

The characteristics of people with this spiritual gift are self-starters, confident, positive, optimistic, analytical and team builders.

The pros and cons of having the gift of administration are listed in the following page:

PROS	CONS
Completes tasks efficiently	Hates wasted time, time, money, or resources
Works tirelessly	Listens more to self than others
Motivates others	Forgets that "I" is not in team
Dedicates him/herself to God	Misses the spiritual importance of the project

What to observe:

The person with the gift of administration is very focused, organized, and knows what the completed project should look like. They hate wasted time, money, and resources. Even though this is the case, those in administration should be sensitive to how this is portrayed to the team. Some waste may be the result of weather, sickness, or a misunderstanding of what was required. Getting to the end without a lot of hurt feelings will be a testament to working together in unity and will certainly glorify God.

Being an expert at something does not give us the right to create an atmosphere where others feel reluctant to raise new and creative options. If there is a sense that only a few people have the best ideas, this will eventually become an issue as the project progresses. For example, if the person with this gift decides to use his architect for the new church building, when it comes time to recommend the construction contractor others may not recommend a church builder because they feel their recommendation won't be taken seriously. But that company could be the best one for the job.

When the person with the gift of administration forgets that "I" is not in "team", they may be surprised when they discover they need the team, but the team will not support them. One person can't do everything. The team is responsible for different areas. If they feel unnecessary or disregarded in other situations, they may use the next opportunity to demonstrate how they can delay an action needed to get to the next phase.

Administrators take pride in leading a project to completion. They love to be able to say the project was completed early and under budget. If the spiritual importance of the project was decimated along the way, it may be necessary to rededicate the project to the Lord. Taking the time to pray at the start, throughout, and at the project's completion will give God glory!

Where to serve:
Persons with this gift find joy and effectiveness in the following and similar types of ministries: Small Groups, Church Administrator, Property Management, Special Projects, and Steward Ministry.

CHAPTER 9

THE GIFT OF MERCY

How will you know if mercy is your gift? You have uncontrollable compassion for those who are in misery, regardless of whether you know them or not. You love easily. You love all people. You have genuine care and concern for people. Your heart breaks to see people suffering.

The New Unger's Bible dictionary defines mercy as:

A form of love determined by the state or condition of its object. Their state is one of suffering and need, while they may be unworthy or ill-deserving. Mercy is at once the disposition of love, respecting such, and the kindly ministry of love for their relief. Mercy is a Christian grace and is very strongly urged toward all men.

A few scriptures in the Bible that refer to mercy are listed below. You should study them and more if you think this may be your gift.

Lamentations 3:22-23 KJV

22 It is of the Lord's mercies that we are not consumed, because his compassions fail not.

23 They are new every morning: great is thy faithfulness.

Matthew 22:36-40 KJV

36 Master, which is the great commandment in the law?
37 Jesus said unto him, Thou shalt love the Lord thy God with all thy heart, and with all thy soul, and with all thy mind.
38 This is the first and great commandment.
39 And the second is like unto it, Thou shalt love thy neighbour as thyself.
40 On these two commandments hang all the law and the prophets.

1 John 3:18 KJV

18 My little children, let us not love in word, neither in tongue; but in deed and in truth.

Luke 6:35-36 KJV

35 But love ye your enemies, and do good, and lend, hoping for nothing again; and your reward shall be great, and ye shall be the children of the Highest: for he is kind unto the unthankful and to the evil.
36 Be ye therefore merciful, as your Father also is merciful.

John 15:17 KJV

17 These things I command you, that ye love one another.

A way to demonstrate mercy is for us to love our enemies or lend to those in need, without expecting something in return. We all know we can't do that on our own. But if we are sincere about making the attempt, God will work in our hearts to transform our feelings into those feelings that can show love to the unlovable and lend to the undeserving, without looking for a reward.

Yet, the reward does come, not from the recipient but from the one who really matters. The reward is great! The reward is to be accepted as God's children. As God's children, we are to demonstrate His character and one of His characteristics is mercy, so be merciful like your Father.

What makes this your gift is that, after hearing about or seeing someone suffering, you must get up and do something. Like the person with the gift of giving, who gives money and resources, the person with the gift of mercy gives of themselves. This person realizes that mercy, like love, is an action word.

People with this gift have a real heart for people, they feel a tenderness toward others, they look for different ways to show kindness and they want to see more love in people they know or don't know, and in the world.

There must be an action that follows mercy to identify the specific need.

The disciple John called himself the one that Jesus loves, so it is no surprise that pastor and bestselling author, Dr. Charles Stanley names him as one in the Bible who exemplifies mercy. Jesus, of course, is the primary person in the Bible who exemplifies mercy. Jesus recognized John as the merciful and compassionate disciple while on the cross.

Jesus turned the care of his mother over to John. What a great honor for John. Who would you ask to care for your mother if you were dying? It would need to be someone who has a heart of mercy.

John writes about Jesus' compassionate and merciful character as he recounts the stories of Nicodemus, the Samaritan woman, the raising of Lazarus, and others. By sharing those stores of mercy, John encourages the people of Bible times and today to believe that Jesus is the Messiah, the Son of God.

Who do you know that is full of mercy and compassion? The people I know with this gift go out of their way to show the love of God by giving of themselves. They may cook for others, care for others, make home repairs, provide services for free, treat others to dinner, etc. The person on the receiving end does not need to be suffering in a grave or serious manner to be a recipient of a merciful servant. In fact, these acts serve to ward off worse conditions.

People with this gift may only share what they do with a close friend. The reason they give of themselves is to give God glory and not to garner glory or praise for themselves. It may be only at a funeral, that you learn of the deeds this person performed as recipients rise to share how he or she helped them through a time of serious need.

People passionate about mercy have likely been the recipient of mercy previously. Having suffered themselves, they know how sharing this gift can turn minds and circumstances around. With help at just the right time, they can conquer a terrible situation and turn it completely around for good. They can see their past self and rejoice as they help someone else overcome a bad hand that life had dealt them.

Persons and situations in the Bible that demonstrate mercy are John, the Prison Warden (toward Joseph), Joshua (toward Rahab), and David (toward Saul).

John. John describes himself as the one Jesus loved so we know he is concerned about mercy.

Mercy is demonstrated through love. John writes more about love than any other writer in the New Testament. There are 39 verses in John, 26 verses in 1 John, 4 verses in 2 John, and 2 verses in 3 John. John tells us that God so loved the world; that God loves the Son; that Jesus loved Martha, Mary, and Lazarus; that we should not love the praise of men; that we are commanded to love one another; and more.

The Prison Warden. Based on the direction from God, the Prison Warden showed lovingkindness to Joseph while he was in prison. Lovingkindness is another way to express mercy. Instead of suffering in prison, Joseph was put over all the other prisoners and managed them in such a way as to relieve the Prison Warden of any worry because he knew God was with Joseph. There are many interesting twists and turns in Joseph's life, many describe it from the pit to the palace. This was just one stop along the way.

Joshua. If you know the story of Rahab, you know that it includes a lesson on mercy. Many describe her as a harlot who owned and managed an inn. When Joshua and Caleb came as spies to Jericho, she knew about their God and believed that they would destroy and take the town. To save herself and her family, she hid them and lied to the officers in search of the spies. Joshua showed her mercy and promised that she and her family would be spared when they returned to capture Jericho.

David. Although David was anointed as the king between the age of 10 and 15, he did not become king until he was 30 years old. Many of the years in between were spent running from King Saul. At first, Saul loved David and called for him to play his harp. Even Saul's son Johnathan loved David. Later, when David became more popular among the people as a conqueror, King Saul became jealous and searched for David to kill him. More than once, David was close enough to King Saul to kill him, but he didn't. He left Saul evidence, so he would know that David had shown him mercy and had not killed him.

The characteristics of people with this gift are compassionate, selfless, hardworking, friendly, lovable, and thoughtful.

The pros and cons of having the gift of mercy are listed below:

PROS	CONS
Understands the need for mercy	Ignores God's purpose for suffering
Shows mercy quickly	Mistakes mercy for sexual desire

Remembers their mercy experiences from the past	Forgets about the need for salvation in the situation
Goes out of their way to demonstrate mercy	Neglects other assignments

What to observe:
The gift of mercy is dependent upon compassion, but it can become a negative concern if we interfere in what God's purpose is for the suffering. The person with this gift wants to help alleviate the pain. Normally, that would be a good thing. It becomes an issue when God is permitting the pain as a trial to get them to obey. As most of us would admit, we may remain in a situation longer than necessary if it were not for the suffering. God always knows what He is doing.

When a person is at their lowest and someone appears to help them of the opposite sex, they may see the intentions to help as a sexual advance. That is why it is a good idea to have another person come along with you to minister mercy. You will need to be very clear of your intentions to help, by referencing scriptures or comparisons to obvious platonic assistance between friends or sisters and brothers in Christ.

We know that we need to meet the basic needs of food, clothing, and shelter before we can really get a person to listen. However, once those needs are met, we need to begin the conversation on how they can avoid returning to their prior predicament by offering them Jesus Christ as Savior. Based on past experiences, one person may be completely ready to take the Romans Road while others may not. The Romans Road is a series of verses in the book of Romans that help walk or direct an unbeliever to the understanding of salvation. They include Rom. 3:23; 6:23; 5:8; and 10:9-10. As stated in 1 Corinthians 3:7, one plants, one waters, but God gives the increase. Pray and ask God to show you where this person is in their walk.

With such beautiful attributes of love and compassion in this gift, it's also important to monitor how many mercy ministries one gets involved in. You are only one person and, though you may feel like you can help many people, it's similar to the gift of serving. If there are too many people for you to help you will become ineffective and overwhelmed. Pray that God will give you discernment on where He wants you to utilize your gift of mercy.

Where to serve:
The person with this gift feels joy and is effective while serving in the following and similar types of ministries: Missions, Deacons, Counseling, Outreach, Special Needs, Homeless, and Prisons.

CHAPTER 10

THE CHALLENGE

You are almost ready to go! Here is your challenge...now that you know your Spiritual Gifts; demonstrate faith, love, forgiveness, commitment, unity, and prayer with your co-laborers.

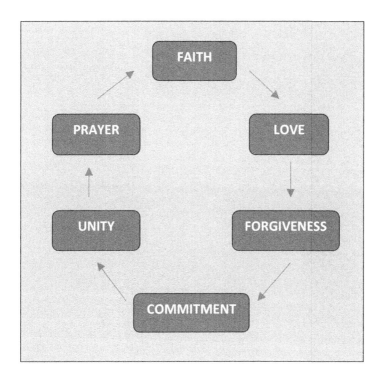

"Take the first step in faith. You don't have to see the whole staircase, just take the first step" (Martin Luther King, Jr.).

So, go forth and glorify God by using the Spiritual Gifts He gave you for His local church and community! And don't forget to serve as Christ would with love, joy, peace, patience, gentleness, goodness, faith, meekness, and self-control, according to Galatians 5:22-23. Amen!

CONCLUDING QUOTE

In conclusion we end this book as we started it -

"Nothing on earth compares to a group of believers in a local church, under the control of the Holy Spirit and using their divinely given gifts to minister to the body. The body then builds itself up in love. When growing in unity, truth and love, a lot of problems take care of themselves, before they become big, because the body is healing itself. A healthy body, working as designed will grow and every member will benefit."

Author Unknown

SELECTED BIBLIOGRAPHY

Blanchard, K. & Hodges P., (2005). *Lead Like Jesus.* New York, NY: MJF Books

Dawson, M. (2017). *The Dash Factor: Where Purpose is Revealed and Destiny is Fulfilled.* Middletown, DE: CreateSpace Independent Publishing Platform.

Evans, T. (2003). *Life Essentials: for Knowing God Better, Experiencing God Deeper and Loving God More.* Chicago, IL: Moody Publishers.

James, E. & Wooten, L. (2010). *Leading Under Pressure: From Surviving to Thriving Before, During, and After a Crisis.* New York, NY: Routledge. Taylor and Frances Group.

Manigault, L. (2013). *The Power of Your Faith: Spiritual Inspirational and Practical Devotions.* North Charleston, SC: CreateSpace Independent Publishing Platform.

Maxwell, J. (2017). *The Power of Significance: How Purpose Changes Your Life.* New York, NY: Center Street.

McDonald, J. (2012). *The Vertical Church: What Every Heart Longs For. What Every Church Can Be.* Colorado Springs, CO: David C. Cook.

McNaughton, D & Wegner, J. (2010). *Learning to Follow Jesus: A Step-by-Step Discipleship Guide.* Spring City, PA: Morning Joy Media.

Rainer, T. (2013). *I Am A Church Member: Discovering the Attitude that Makes a Difference.* Nashville, TN: B&H Publishing Group.

Ross, T. (2015). *A Servant's Heart: 180 Encouraging Thoughts for Church Volunteers* Uhrichsville, OH: Barbour Publishing, Inc.

Scott, S. (2009). *The Greatest Man Who Ever Lived: Secrets for Unparalleled Success and Unshakable Happiness from the Life of Jesus.* Colorado Springs, CO: WaterBrook Press.

Sinek, S. (2009). *Start With Why: How Great Leaders Inspire Everyone to Take Action.* New York, NY: Portfolio/Penguin Group.

Stanley, C. (1999). *Ministering Through Spiritual Gifts.* Nashville, TN: Thomas Nelson, Inc.

Unger, M. (2006). *The New Unger's Bible Dictionary.* Chicago, IL: Moody Publishers.

Made in the USA
Monee, IL
13 July 2021